SPIDERS!

STRANGE AND WONDERFUL

Laurence Pringle

Illustrated by
Meryl Henderson

BOYDS MILLS PRESS
AN IMPRINT OF HIGHLIGHTS
Honesdale, Pennsylvania

For my daughter Rebecca—smart, compassionate, witty, and brave. She sees the best in people, dogs, and cats, and may someday see the best in spiders.
—LP

To Ellen Mahnken, a dear friend and the most multitalented, adventurous artist I know.
—MH

The author thanks Dr. Norman I. Platnick, Senior Scientist and Peter J. Solomon Family Curator Emeritus of Spiders, Division of Invertebrate Zoology, American Museum of Natural History, New York, New York, for his careful review of the text and illustrations.

Boyds Mills Press
An Imprint of Highlights
815 Church Street
Honesdale, Pennsylvania 18431
boydsmillspress.com
Printed in China

ISBN: 978-1-62979-321-4
Library of Congress Control Number: 2016959818

First edition
Production by Sue Cole
The text of this book is set in Goudy Oldstyle.
The illustrations are done in watercolor and pencil.

10 9 8 7 6 5 4 3 2 1

As you read these words, there is probably a spider nearby.

In fact, there may be several spiders close to you. One may lurk under a chair. Another hides in the corner of a window. Oh, and there may be one in a little silk web, up by the ceiling.

These spiders want nothing to do with you. To them, you are a huge, dangerous monster. Your spider companions just want to go on with their quiet, amazing lives.

Spiders live just about everywhere. Only one continent is spider-free. Currently, Antarctica is too cold for spiders to survive. However, as Earth's climate warms, spiders may also be able to live on Antarctica.

On all other continents and on nearly every bit of land, spiders thrive. They live on ocean beaches, and also high on Mount Everest, 22,000 feet above sea level. Spiders live in Arctic tundra, deserts, prairies, jungles, farm fields, and in the parks, gardens, and backyards of every city and town. Some live high in treetops, others deep in caves. Some can even live underwater. And sometimes tiny spiders sail overhead. Up in the sky, winds can carry their lightweight bodies many miles. They alight and find new living places, perhaps near—or in—your home.

Dwarf spider

Wandering spider from
Central America

Goldenrod (crab)
spider on a
prairie rose

Sand-dune-running
crab spider

5

Spiders are **arachnids**. They are part of a huge animal group that includes mites, ticks, scorpions, and daddy longlegs (all shown much larger than actual size). You can usually tell an arachnid from an insect by counting legs. Insects have six (three pairs), and spiders have eight (four pairs). Also, many insects have antennae and wings. Spiders don't.

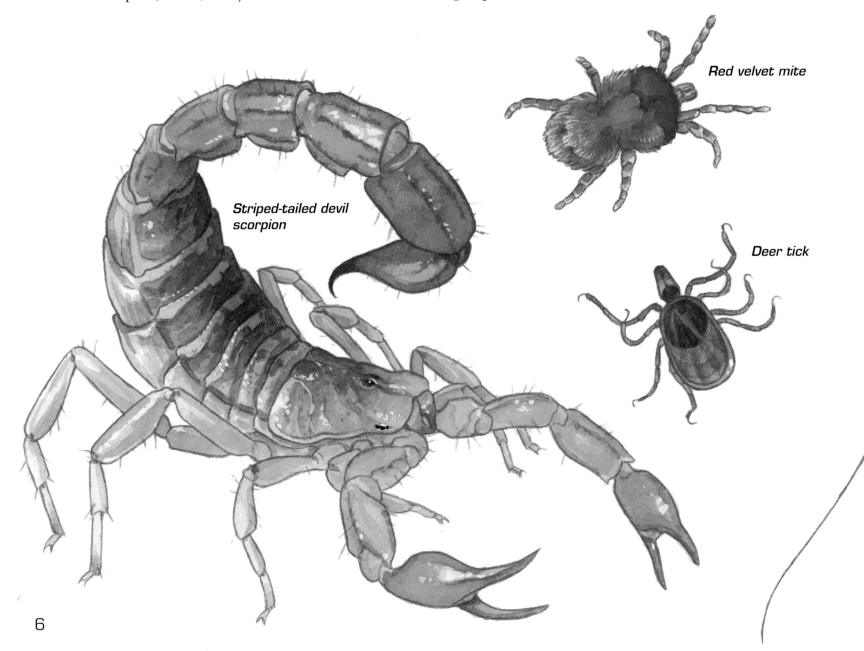

Red velvet mite

Striped-tailed devil scorpion

Deer tick

Brown daddy longlegs

Spiders and other arachnids have flourished on Earth for about 380 million years. We know this from studying **fossils**. Imprints of spider bodies have been found in ancient rocks that formed long ago in China. However, spider bodies lack bones or other hard parts, so only a few become fossils in rocks. Most spider fossils form after a spider gets trapped in sticky tree sap (resin), which slowly becomes hard, clear **amber**. Well-preserved spiders can be seen in amber from long-ago times: 20, 40, 90, and even 125 million years ago.

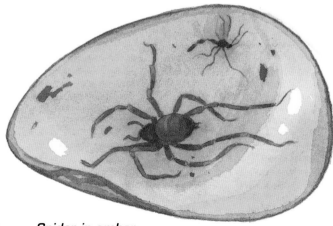

Spider fossil in stone   *Spider in amber*

Our planet swarms with spiders! So far, 46,000 kinds (species) of spiders have been identified. Even though some spiders have leg spans as large as dinner plates, most are much smaller. Some are not much bigger than the period at the end of this sentence. No wonder scientists believe there are many other spider species—perhaps more than 100,000—that haven't been discovered yet.

With so many spider species in the world, using common names to describe them can be confusing. People in different parts of the world might use different words for the same species. For instance, in Spain, spiders that people call *tarantulas* are actually wolf spiders. They are *not* related to the big spiders of North, South, and Central America that are also called tarantulas. Similarly, the term *jumping spider* can refer to any of more than 5,000 different species. For this reason, it is important for every species to have a scientific name that can be used worldwide.

Below, the scientific classification of one kind of spider is shown. Also, the three main groups of all kinds of spiders are shown on the next page.

Zebra spider

Classifying a Spider

To better understand how living things are related to one another, scientists study their characteristics closely. This helps to arrange all living things in different groups. Of course, new discoveries can lead to changes that make the system more accurate.

To the right is how one kind of jumping spider is classified, beginning with the fact that it is an animal.

Kingdom	Animal
Subkingdom	Metazoa (many-celled animals)
Phylum	**Arthropoda** (animals with jointed limbs and no inner skeletons, including insects, crabs, and spiders)
Class	Arachnida (including spiders, ticks, mites)
Order	Araneae (all spiders)
Suborder	Araneomorphae (the biggest group of spiders)
Family	Salticidae (all jumping spiders)
Genus	*Salticus* (including a number of closely related jumping spiders)
Species	*scenicus* (one kind of spider in the *Salticus* genus)

In Latin, the word *saltus* means "a leap." This spider's name is *Salticus scenicus*. Sometimes called the zebra spider, it lives in North America and northern Europe.

Mesothelae

There are fewer than 100 species of Mesothelae (one shown to the left). They live in Southeast Asia and are sometimes called "living fossils" because they are very similar to Earth's earliest spiders. Unlike other spiders, the tops of their **abdomens** are covered by hard plates arranged like segments.

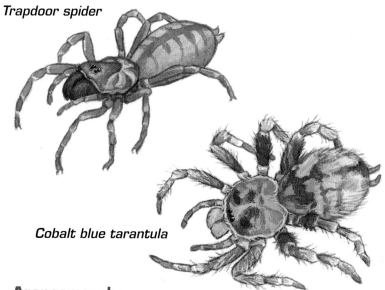

Trapdoor spider

Mygalomorphs

These spiders usually have two pairs of lungs, and fangs that strike downward, instead of from the sides, like most other spiders. They include trapdoor spiders and the biggest spiders of all, tarantulas.

Cobalt blue tarantula

Wolf spider

Araneomorphs

These spiders usually have one pair of lungs, with a system of tubes that carry oxygen to organs. Their jaws open and close sideways. They make up 90 percent of all spiders, including wolf spiders, jumping spiders, orb weavers, crab spiders, fishing spiders, and many more. A few are shown here, and there are many others throughout this book.

Jumping spider

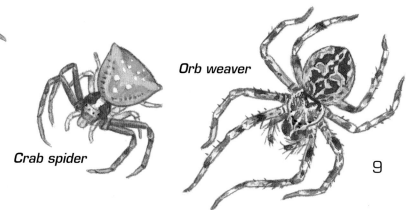

Orb weaver

Fishing spider

Crab spider

9

Spiders vary a lot, in their color, the length of their legs, and the size of their bodies and eyes. However, all spiders are made up of two main sections: an abdomen and a **cephalothorax**, shown here with other key body parts.

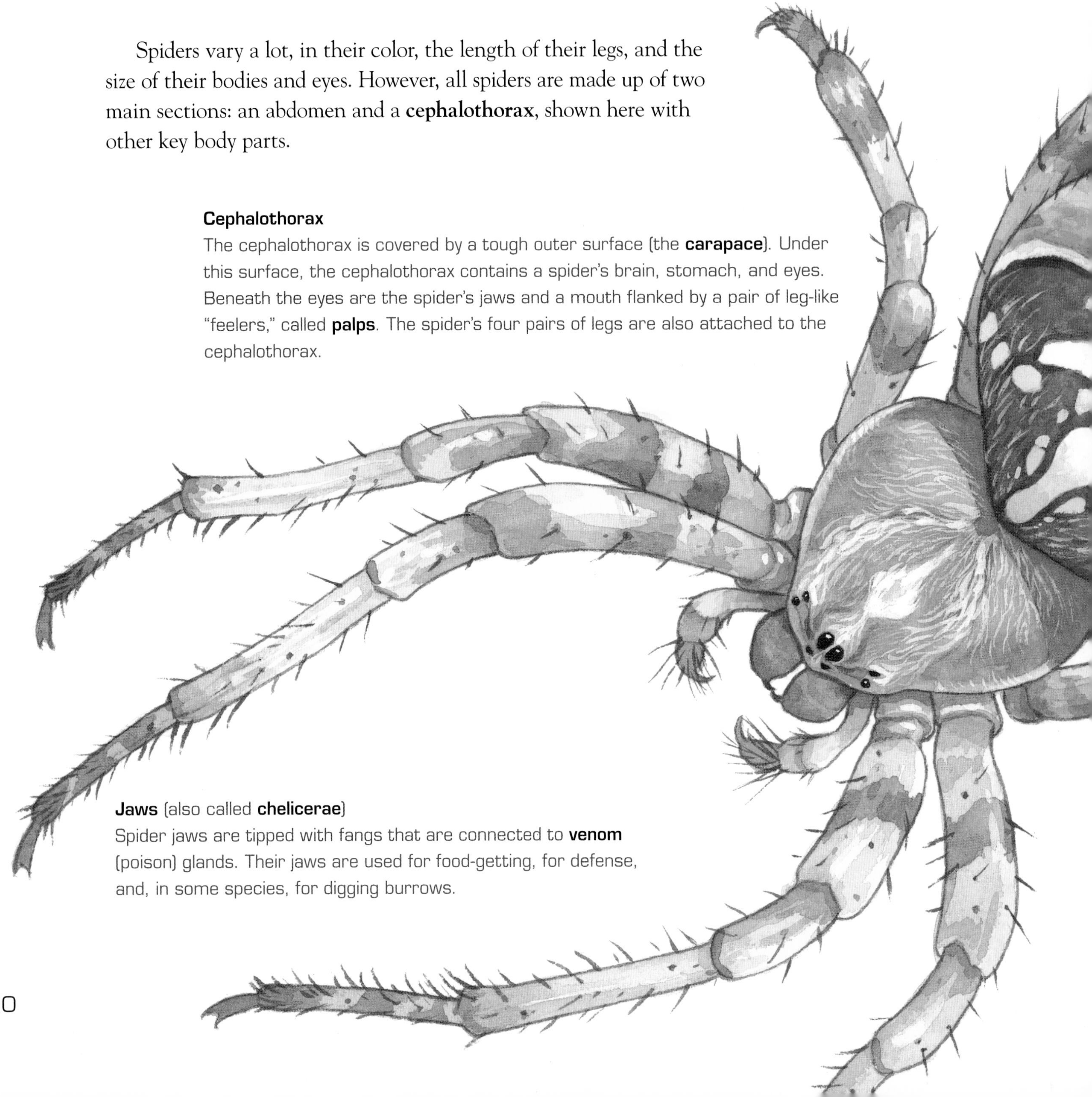

Cephalothorax

The cephalothorax is covered by a tough outer surface (the **carapace**). Under this surface, the cephalothorax contains a spider's brain, stomach, and eyes. Beneath the eyes are the spider's jaws and a mouth flanked by a pair of leg-like "feelers," called **palps**. The spider's four pairs of legs are also attached to the cephalothorax.

Jaws (also called **chelicerae**)

Spider jaws are tipped with fangs that are connected to **venom** (poison) glands. Their jaws are used for food-getting, for defense, and, in some species, for digging burrows.

Abdomen

A spider's abdomen contains the **silk glands,** the heart, much of the digestive tract, the reproductive system, and the breathing apparatus, called **book lungs**. (Located just inside the bottom of a spider's abdomen, they look somewhat like the stacked pages of a book.) At the very tip of the abdomen are **spinnerets** (from two to eight in number), from which silk flows.

Garden spider

Legs

Eight in number, spider legs are tipped with claws that are specially adapted to hold on tight to prey, the silky strands of a web, the underside of a leaf, or even to a wall. The legs are also covered with sensory hairs, spines, and slits that detect touch, vibrations, and scents in the air.

If a spider could list its basic goals, they would be: stay safe, get food, find a mate. This seems simple enough, but a spider's world is a dangerous place. Most spiders are small. They have no armor. They can be killed by birds, lizards, wasps, and other predators, and even by their own relatives, bigger spiders. Sometimes spiders are attacked by humans with their terrible weapons—massive feet, brooms, vacuum cleaners, and poison sprays.

Spider senses, especially smell and touch, can help them to avoid being killed and to get food and seek mates. Most spiders have eight eyes, arranged in two or three rows. The eyes usually look outward at different angles, so spiders can see all around. Eight eyes may seem like plenty, but most spiders don't see very well. Their small eyes do not see details clearly. Mostly they detect motion. Spiders that are active hunters, such as jumping spiders and wolf spiders, have two eyes that are larger and have sharper vision than the other six.

Jumping spider face

Wolf spider face

Spider eyes and their arrangement vary a lot from species to species. (In fact, when scientists try to identify a spider, its eye arrangement is key evidence.) Though most spiders have eight, some have six eyes or fewer. Spiders living in the darkness of caves may have no eyes at all. Spiders with poor vision (or no eyes) depend on other senses.

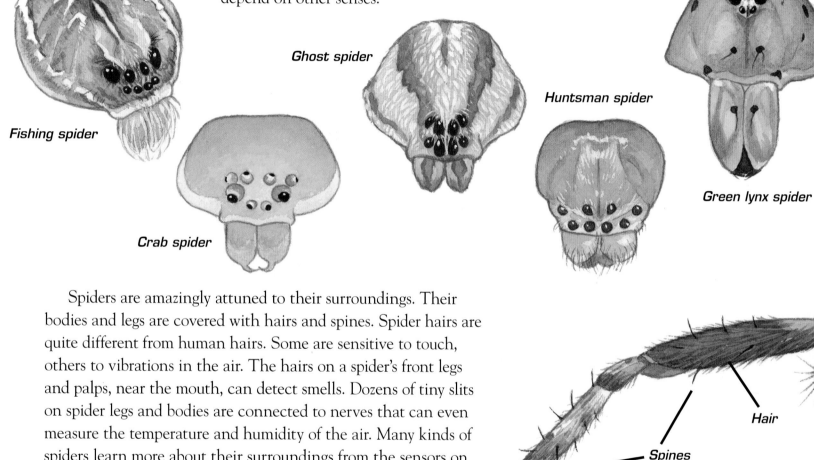

Fishing spider

Crab spider

Ghost spider

Huntsman spider

Green lynx spider

Hair

Spines

Metatarsus

Tarsus

Claw

Spiders are amazingly attuned to their surroundings. Their bodies and legs are covered with hairs and spines. Spider hairs are quite different from human hairs. Some are sensitive to touch, others to vibrations in the air. The hairs on a spider's front legs and palps, near the mouth, can detect smells. Dozens of tiny slits on spider legs and bodies are connected to nerves that can even measure the temperature and humidity of the air. Many kinds of spiders learn more about their surroundings from the sensors on their legs than from their eyes!

13

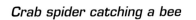

Crab spider catching a bee

Imagine that you are a little spider. To eat, you need to kill insects. Some of them are bigger and stronger than you are. Your body is not armored, and your jaws are not strong. In a struggle, you could easily get injured or killed. To survive, you need a special weapon.

Spiders have that weapon: venom. Almost every spider species has glands that can send a dose of venom to the tips of its fangs. With this venom, a spider can kill prey that is much bigger than itself. A little crab spider can wait on a flower, then ambush a bumblebee. The spider gives one quick, venomous bite. Soon the small spider has a big meal.

The venom of many kinds of spiders does not actually kill an animal. Instead the prey is paralyzed. It can't move. Whether the prey is dead or paralyzed, spiders usually begin to feed right away. Most spiders do not chew their food. Some species have chemicals within their venom that start to digest parts of an insect's body. All species release fluids from their stomachs that begin digestion. Most of the inner parts of an insect's body become a soup that is slurped up by the spider.

Spiders conserve their venom. Small prey gets only a small dose. And when a spider faces a really big animal, it often defends itself with a dry bite, not wasting venom.

Cutaway view, inside a spider's jaw, or chelicerae

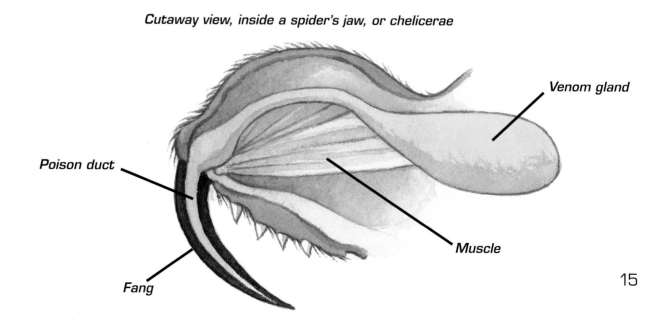

Venom gland

Poison duct

Muscle

Fang

15

No spider ever wants to bite a human. However, when it is surprised and can't escape, it may try to bite. Even then, most spiders are harmless. Often their jaws are too small or weak to break through human skin. Even when a spider is able to inject some venom into skin, it usually has little or no effect. Scientists have learned that most "spider bites" that people report are actually skin infections, or bites or stings from insects or ticks.

A few kinds of spiders do have venom that can harm humans. Some are shown on these pages. Several dozen species (out of 46,000) can give a dangerous bite. Spider venoms contain complex mixes of chemicals. One harmful kind of venom can cause wounds that heal very slowly and leave scars. The other dangerous kind can affect an animal's nervous system. It can cause pain that spreads through the body and can even cause a person to stop breathing. However, deaths from spider bites are rare. Many hospitals have medicines on hand (called **antivenins**) that are specially suited to treat the bad effects of dangerous spider venom.

Black widows are the best-known of several related species in North America, including the brown widow and the northern widow, and others around the world (including the katipo spider of New Zealand). Widow spiders are small and shy. Male widow spiders are tiny and do not bite.

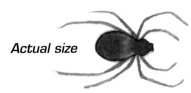

Actual size

Female black widow, with red hourglass figure on underside of abdomen

Brown recluse spiders of North and South America (right) are related to other recluse species in the world. (*Recluse* means "shy.") The six-eyed sand spider is a crab-shaped relative of recluse spiders. It has powerful venom but rarely encounters people in its desert home of southern Africa and South America.

Female brown recluse

Actual size

Male funnel-web

Funnel-web spiders of Australia (left) have big fangs and powerful venom. The venom of males is more dangerous than that of females.

Actual size

The Brazilian wandering spider (right) is big, with dangerous venom, and unusual spider behavior: bold, not shy.

Actual size

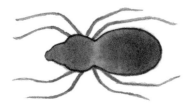

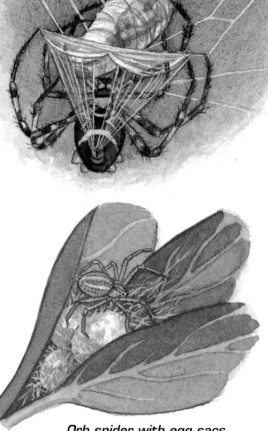

Silver **Argiope** *wrapping prey*

Every kind of spider has silk glands. These little chemical factories in a spider's abdomen can produce as many as seven different kinds of silk. The silk, in liquid form, flows to the spinnerets at a spider's rear end. As tiny strands of silk reach a spinneret opening, they change chemically and form a single solid thread. The spider uses the claws and hairs of its two rear legs to pull the silk out.

Scientists wish that they could easily make something as extraordinary as spider silk. A strand of lightweight spider silk is stronger than a strand of steel of the same size. Spider silk can be stretched up to three times its length without breaking. Many kinds of songbirds know the value of spider silk. They gather it from webs and use this soft but tough material when building their nests.

Some spider webs are big and showy, but webs can also be small. They come in a variety of shapes: domes, tunnels, funnels, bowls, sheets, or just a complex mess of threads. Thousands of spider species make no webs at all. They use their silk in other ways—for example, to wrap up prey to save for a later meal, or to protect eggs in a silken sac. Some other uses of silk are shown on these pages.

Orb spider with egg sacs

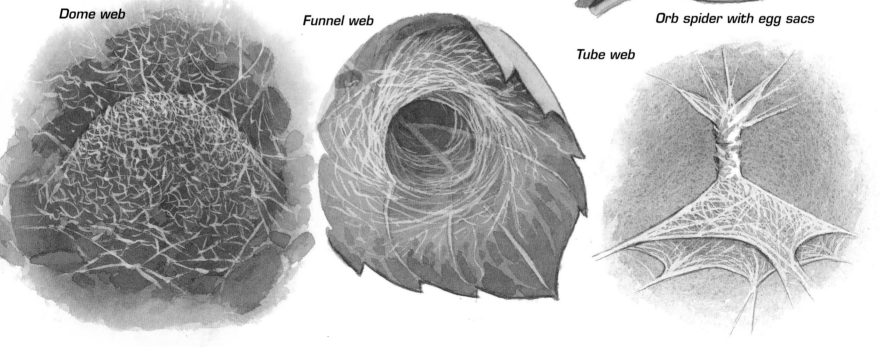

Dome web

Funnel web

Tube web

On the move or at rest, many spiders lay down a strong **dragline**. It can be a life-saving thread. When a spider falls or jumps, it can quickly climb back up its dragline.

Jumping spider, Phlegra *genus*

The water, or diving bell, spider of Britain, northern Europe, and Asia spends nearly all of its life underwater. It spins a silken home filled with oxygen, attached to an underwater plant. The shelter is sometimes called a diving bell. When its home needs more oxygen, the spider swims up to the surface. Dense hairs on its body trap air, which becomes air bubbles when the spider returns to its hideout. Water spiders catch prey underwater, and even raise their young within their diving bell shelter.

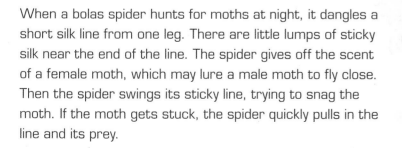

Bolas spider

When a bolas spider hunts for moths at night, it dangles a short silk line from one leg. There are little lumps of sticky silk near the end of the line. The spider gives off the scent of a female moth, which may lure a male moth to fly close. Then the spider swings its sticky line, trying to snag the moth. If the moth gets stuck, the spider quickly pulls in the line and its prey.

Water, or diving bell, spider

Ask people to draw a spider web, and most will make a big circle with lines that spread outward from its center like the spokes of a bicycle wheel. This is an **orb web**, a beautiful spider creation, especially when bejeweled with rain or dewdrops. The beloved spider named Charlotte made orb webs in the classic story *Charlotte's Web*.

Orb webs are designed as death traps for flying insects. They may be built in the evening to catch night-flying insects. Some kinds of spiders spin their webs near dawn, preparing to catch insects that are active in daytime. Orb webs are made by female spiders and juvenile males. Most adult male spiders are not web-builders; they wander, searching for mates.

A spider starts by making the highest part of its web. From a high point, it releases a line of lightweight silk. The line floats a little way, perhaps helped by a breeze, and catches on a twig or other support. This creates a bridge. The spider then goes back and forth on the bridge, adding tough dragline silk. The drawings on this page show how a spider adds other lines to make a strong framework, including threads that look like the spokes of a wheel. Then, beginning in the center, it goes round and round in ever-bigger circles. Finally, the spider lays down some lines of glue-coated silk. The spider knows to avoid these lines so it doesn't get stuck in its own web.

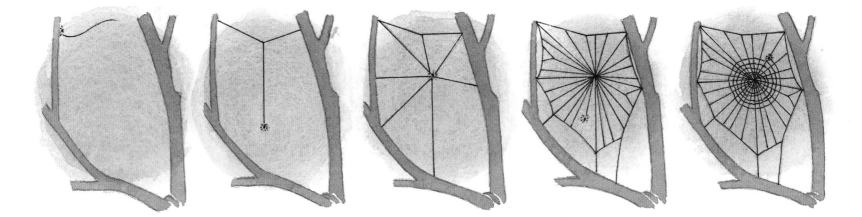

Many orb webs are small, less than a foot across. Among the largest of all are webs made by the *Nephila* spiders of the tropics. They can be five feet wide and capture bats, which the spiders eat.

Some kinds of spiders wait in the center of their web, alert for prey to be caught. Others lurk to the side. An Australian spider makes its orb web, then weaves in a leaf that curls up as it dries. The spider hides within the leaf.

Orb weavers don't see well, so they stay in constant contact with their web. Their super-sensitive sense of touch alerts them to vibrations. They can detect vibrations caused by a captured insect, or a different vibration from a possible mate. They can also sense when their web needs repair. Many orb weavers build a new web every day. And some species recycle. They eat and digest the old silk, which then becomes part of brand-new threads.

Nephila *spider*

21

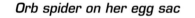

Orb spider on her egg sac

Wolf spider carrying her young

When a male spider finds a female's web, he usually taps a line with a coded signal. Making the wrong kind of vibration can be a fatal mistake. Males of most spider species are much smaller than females. A male spider can become a meal for the female, even if she first mates with him.

Some kinds of female spiders produce only a few eggs. Others lay many hundreds. Usually the mother spider encloses the eggs in a protective sac made of silk. Some species guard these egg sacs, and some—including wolf spiders— even watch over their young after they hatch. In most species, however, the **spiderlings** are totally on their own. They look like tiny, pale adults. As soon as they hatch they are hungry, and they attack any small moving creature. It might be their own sister or brother.

22

Spiderlings that get away from their siblings have a chance of surviving. One way to do this is **ballooning**. A spiderling lets out a lightweight line of silk. The slightest breeze can lift the silk, and the spiderling, up, up, and away. Small adult spiders can also travel this way. Ballooning spiders have landed on ships at sea, hundreds of miles from the nearest land.

If a spiderling survives and finds food, it soon needs to grow bigger. Spiders grow by **molting**, shedding their old **exoskeletons** and emerging with new, bigger ones. Each molt produces a whole set of eight legs, too, replacing any that were lost. In its life, which is often just a few months, a spider may molt up to a dozen times.

Spiderlings ballooning

23

Nearly all spiders are alike in some ways—for example, producing silk and venom. In other ways, however, they are amazingly different. The six spiders shown on these pages all have unusual ways to get food, or to avoid becoming food.

The abdomen of the arrow-shaped thorn spider of the Americas (left) has a scary shape. Two big sharp-looking spines point backward, and two smaller spines point forward. As it waits for prey in its orb web, this spider looks unappealing to birds and other predators.

With its legs tucked in, out of sight, the bird-dropping spider of Africa (right) looks like a wet glob of bird poop. Predators avoid it. The spider sits on a leaf, emits a scent that attracts flies, and waits for a meal to arrive.

The golden wheel spider (left) hides in burrows by day and hunts at night in the Namib Desert of southern Africa. It tends to live on steep slopes of sand dunes and has an unusual way of escaping predators. When a wasp attacks, the spider folds its legs up and hurls itself downslope. It can roll at great speed, disappearing from the wasp's view.

24

The grass-stem running crab spider (right) lurks in wet meadows in parts of Europe and North America. Gripping a grass blade with its slim body and long legs, it blends in well. When an insect comes near, the spider leaps upon it or swiftly chases it through the grass jungle.

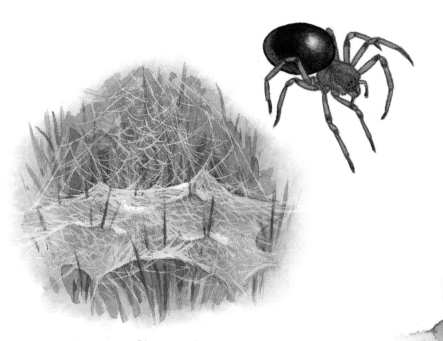

Dwarf spiders (left), also called hammock-web spiders, make up a huge spider family, with many species in Europe and hundreds more in North America. They spin small sheet webs in fields and meadows. The webs may go unnoticed until they are festooned with raindrops or dewdrops. Then hundreds of webs can be revealed. The spiders hang upside down beneath their webs and attack from below, biting prey through the silken sheet.

Sheet web

Trapdoor spiders (right), related to tarantulas, dig tube-like burrows in the ground with their jaws. These hideouts are usually lined with silk. Layers of silk and soil make the door, which is usually hinged on one side. To keep intruders out, a spider holds the door shut with its claws and fangs. At night the door is left slightly ajar, and the spider waits with its front legs sticking out, ready to grab passing prey.

25

When people think of scary spiders, they often imagine big hairy tarantulas, which are mostly harmless to humans. They can be fascinating pets. In fact, some kinds of tarantulas are now scarce in the wild because so many have been caught to be sold in pet shops. Captive female tarantulas have lived more than twenty years.

About thirty kinds of tarantulas live in the United States, mostly in the Southwest. In all, there are more than nine hundred kinds around the world. In Africa they are called baboon or monkey spiders; in Southeast Asia they are called ground tigers. The biggest of all, called the Goliath birdeater, lives in South America. Its legs span nearly twelve inches, measured from the tip of one outstretched leg to the tip of the opposite leg. Despite its name, this tarantula is no threat to adult birds, although it can catch prey as big as mice and frogs.

Mexican red-knee tarantula

Goliath birdeater tarantula

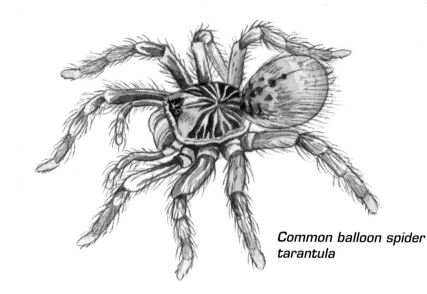
Common balloon spider tarantula

Indian black and white tarantula

Tarantulas don't see well. They rely on the sensory hairs on their bodies and legs to detect vibrations. Usually they are nighttime "sit and wait" predators. Some species live in trees and bushes, but most hide in silk-lined burrows that they dig with their big jaws. Those same jaws can grab and crush prey when a tarantula strikes from its lair.

A tarantula may defend itself by using its rear legs to kick a shower of barbed hairs from its abdomen. This can irritate people's eyes or cause an itchy skin rash, so pet tarantulas are handled gently, or not at all.

27

Some jumping spider faces

The words *cute*, *delightful*, and *charming* are rarely used to describe spiders—but they might be if jumping spiders were bigger and easier to see. Jumping spiders are small, many less than a quarter of an inch long.

Like most spiders, jumpers have six small eyes and two large ones. But their big eyes are unusual. They are larger and more complex than most spider eyes. They give jumping spiders an owl-like look and the best eyesight of all spiders. Jumpers use their keen vision to avoid enemies and also to see, stalk, and attack prey. They hunt in daylight. To catch food, they can leap as far as thirty times their own body length. Some jump into the air to grab flying insects!

Some jumping spiders are masters of camouflage and can look exactly like a patch of tree bark. One species of jumping spider from Sri Lanka is called a mimic jumper because it looks, and acts, like an ant. Its two front legs are shaped like ant antennae. The spider holds these legs out in front of its cephalothorax, just as an ant's antennae stick out from the front of its head.

Camouflaged jumper

Ant mimic jumper

Jumping spiders can be as colorful as birds or butterflies. Just as male birds show off their bright colors to attract mates, male jumpers can put on a dazzling display for female spiders. Some kinds dance about, waving their gaudy legs and palps. Male peacock jumping spiders of Australia are especially showy. They raise their brightly colored abdomens, like a peacock's tail feathers, and perform a tiny but spectacular show.

More jumping spiders

Male peacock jumper

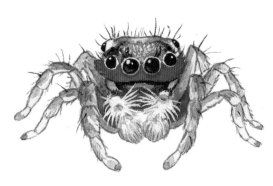

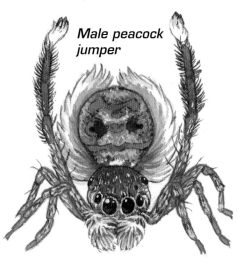

29

Blue mud dauber wasp paralyzing a shamrock spider

Spiders have countless enemies. They include many humans, of course, and other spiders, but also birds, lizards, toads, frogs, centipedes, and predatory insects. Spider-hunting wasps are a big threat. A female tarantula hawk wasp stings a tarantula, paralyzing it, then lays an egg on it. The larva that hatches from the egg then feeds on the spider's body. Mud dauber wasps do the same. They may collect twenty or more small spiders to provide food for their young.

All over the world, spiders are part of food chains, both as prey and as predators. They kill more insects than birds do. Of course, they kill both beneficial insects and pests, but they are still considered strong allies of farmers and gardeners. And spiders are valued in other ways, too. Scientists study some chemicals in spider venom as possible sources of medicines for people. And researchers continue to dream of mass-producing materials as remarkably lightweight and strong as spider silk.

Most people know very little about spiders and may fear them. Just the sight of a harmless species scares some people. This strong fear is called **arachnophobia**.

When people learn about spiders, their fears can diminish—or disappear. An Australian woman named Lynne Kelly often had nightmares about spiders. Still, she decided to study them, in a cautious way. She felt it was safe to watch some spiders through her kitchen window. Over a few months she observed them making webs and catching insects. She was fascinated. When a bird came by and ate every single spider, Lynne was upset.

She was on her way to becoming an **arachnophile**, a person who likes spiders. Eventually she wrote a book, *Spiders: Learning to Love Them*. This all happened because of a simple step: watching spiders as they went about their quiet, amazing lives.

Glossary

Abdomen—The rear main part of a spider's body.

Amber—Tree resin that over time becomes rock-hard. Spiders and insects trapped in resin are sometimes preserved and visible in the amber.

Antivenins—Medicines used to treat the bad effects of dangerous bites of spiders and other venomous animals.

Arachnids—A class of animals that have eight legs and no wings, antennae, or inner skeleton. Arachnids include spiders, scorpions, mites, ticks, and harvestmen (also called daddy longlegs).

Arachnophile—A person who likes spiders and has little or no fear of them.

Arachnophobia—A great fear of all spiders. People with such fears are arachnophobes.

Arthropods—The largest group of all animals on Earth, including all those with jointed legs and a tough outer skeleton. Arthropods include insects, crustaceans, and arachnids.

Ballooning—Travel through the air by small spiders. The spiders release lightweight silken threads that are lifted and carried by rising air and winds.

Book lungs—Breathing organs of spiders, located in the front underside of their abdomens.

Carapace—The tough outer covering of the front part of a spider's body, its cephalothorax.

Cephalothorax—The front part of a spider's body, a combination of its head and thorax.

Chelicerae—Spider jaws, tipped with fangs that can inject venom.

Dragline—A strong silk line glued down as a spider rests or moves. If the spider falls or jumps, it can scramble back up its dragline.

Exoskeleton—The tough outer body covering of spiders and other arthropods, which lack inner skeletons.

Fossils—Skeletons, footprints, and other traces of animals and plants, preserved in rocks that formed long ago. See also **amber**.

Molting—The process of a spider shedding its old exoskeleton to emerge with a new, larger one. In order to grow in size, a spider may molt as many as a dozen times.

Orb webs—Spider webs with silk lines arranged like the spokes of a bicycle wheel and other lines that spiral round and round within the spoke pattern.

Palps—Leg-like feelers in front of a spider's legs, also called pedipalps.

Silk glands—Organs at the rear of a spider's abdomen that can produce up to seven kinds of silk.

Spiderling—A spider newly hatched from its egg.

Spinnerets—Tubes at the rear of a spider's abdomen that emit silk threads.

Venom—Poison produced by spiders that can paralyze or kill insects and other prey.

To Learn More

Books and periodicals

Bishop, Nic. *Spiders*. New York: Scholastic, 2007.

Bradley, Richard. *Common Spiders of North America*. Oakland, CA: University of California Press, 2012.

Dalton, Stephen. *Spiders: The Ultimate Predators*. Buffalo, NY: Firefly, 2011.

Facklam, Margery. *Spiders and Their Web Sites*. Boston: Little, Brown, 2006.

Hillyard, Paul. *The Private Life of Spiders*. Princeton, NJ: Princeton University Press, 2007.

Kelly, Lynne. *Spiders: Learning to Love Them*. Crows Nest, Australia: Jacana Books, 2009.

Lasky, Kathryn. *Silk and Venom: Searching for a Dangerous Spider*. Somerville, MA: Candlewick, 2011.

Montgomery, Sy. *The Tarantula Scientist*. Boston: Houghton Mifflin, 2004.

Shahan, Thomas. "Spiders in Focus." *National Geographic*, December 2011.

Summers, Adam. "Nice Threads." *Natural History*, October 2006, pp. 24–25.

Websites*

www.kidzone.ws/lw/spiders/facts.htm. Basic information about spiders (bodies, uses of silk, venom, etc.).

www.spiderzrule.com. An excellent source of spider information, illustrated with many photographs, including spider fossils in amber.

www.youtube.com/watch?v=d_yYC5r8xMl. Close-up film, set to music, of a male peacock jumping spider courting a female, with leg-waving and colorful display.

*Websites active at time of publication.